NATURAL WORLD

GRIZZLY BEAR

HABITATS • LIFE CYCLES • FOOD CHAINS • THREATS

Michael Leach

HODDER
Wayland

an imprint of Hodder
Children's Books

WWF

Produced in Association with WWF-UK

NATURAL WORLD

Chimpanzee • Crocodile • Dolphin • Elephant • Giant Panda
Great White Shark • Grizzly Bear • Hippopotamus
Killer Whale • Lion • Orangutan • Penguin • Polar Bear • Tiger

Produced for Hodder Wayland by
Roger Coote Publishing
Gissing's Farm, Fressingfield
Suffolk IP21 5SH, UK

WWF is a registered charity no. 201707
WWF-UK, Panda House, Weyside Park
Godalming, Surrey GU7 1XR

Cover: Face to face with a grizzly bear.
Title page: A curious grizzly stands high on its back legs to get a better view of the photographer.
Contents page: At full stretch a grizzly measures up to 2.7 metres high.
Index page: The humped back of this bear shows that it is a grizzly.

Series editor: Polly Goodman
Designer: Victoria Webb

Published in Great Britain in 2000 by Hodder Wayland
an imprint of Hodder Children's Books

A Catalogue record for this book is available from the British Library.

ISBN 0 7502 2875 X

Printed and bound in Belgium by Proost N.V.

Hodder Children's Books
A division of Hodder Headline Ltd
338 Euston Road, London NW1 3BH

Picture acknowledgements
Biofotos 3 (Heather Angel), 15 (Heather Angel), 16 (Heather Angel); Bruce Coleman Collection 7 (Werner Layer), 9 (Leonard Lee Rue), 19 (Joe McDonald), 29 (Joe McDonald), 30 (Stephen J Krasemann), 31 (Johnny Johnson), 34 (Johnny Johnson), 38 (Joe McDonald), 39 (Erwin & Peggy Bauer), 44 top (Leonard Lee Rue), 45 middle (Erwin & Peggy Bauer); Michael Leach 13, 36, 41; Oxford Scientific Films 6 (Judd Cooney), 17 (Tom Ulrich), 18 (Frank Huber), 27 (Stouffer Productions /Animals Animals), 37 (Daniel J Cox), 43 (Daniel J Cox); Stock Market 14 (Kennan Ward), 22 (Ron Sanford), 24 (Tom Brakefield), 32 (Kennan Ward), 33 (Ron Sanford), 44 bottom (Kennan Ward); Tony Stone Images *front cover* (Stephen J Krasemann), 1 (Tim Davis), 10 Paul Souders), 11 (James Balog), 12–13 (Kathy Bushue), 20 (Daniel J Cox), 20–21 (Tom Ulrich), 22–3 (David Myers), 26 (John Warden), 28 (Barbara Filet), 35 (Darrell Gulin), 40 (Kim Heacox), 42 (James Balog), 44 middle (Paul Souders), 45 top (Tom Ulrich), 45 bottom (Kim Heacox), 48 (Daniel J Cox). Map on page 4 by Victoria Webb. All other artworks by Michael Posen.

Contents

Meet the Grizzly

A fully grown grizzly bear is one of the world's most powerful animals. Grizzlies may look slow and clumsy, but they can move quickly and can be very dangerous when angry. The grizzly is a type of brown bear. Its close relative, the European brown bear, can still be found in parts of Europe and Asia. Grizzly bears once lived all over North America, but today they exist only in Alaska, Canada and just a few remote parts of the American Rocky Mountains.

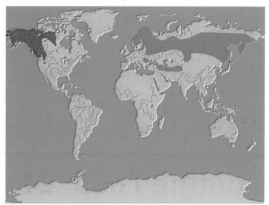

▲ The red shading on this map shows where grizzly bears live in North America. European brown bears are found in the areas shaded green.

GRIZZLY BEAR FACTS

A fully grown grizzly can grow up to 2.1 metres long and 1.3 metres high at the shoulder. Males (known as boars) can weigh up to 362 kilograms. Females (or sows) weigh up to 227 kilograms.

●

The grizzly got its name from its silver-tipped hairs, which can look as though they are covered in frost. In the past, 'grizzly' meant 'frosty'.

●

The grizzly's scientific name is *Ursus arctos horribilis*, which means 'terrible northern bear'.

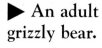
▶ **An adult
grizzly bear.**

Nose
Grizzly bears have an excellent
sense of smell and can locate
food over a huge distance.

Colour
Grizzly bears are
usually brown, but
they can be many
other colours from
cream and dark-yellow
to black.

Claws
Each foot has five sharp
claws, which are used
for digging, breaking
open logs, tearing food
apart and climbing.

Ears
Grizzlies have good hearing.

Eyes
Grizzlies have poor eyesight.
They are short-sighted and have
difficulty identifying objects
more than 9 metres away.

Teeth
Grizzlies have teeth that
help them eat a big
variety of food,
including long canine
teeth and flat molars.

Fur
Each hair on a grizzly bear
has a very light tip, which
makes it look as if it is
covered in frost. This colour
gave the bear its nickname
of 'silvertip'.

Legs
A grizzly standing on its
back legs is around
2.2 metres tall. When
grizzlies stand up on their
hind legs they are not
usually being aggressive.
It is more likely that they
are curious and are simply
trying to get a better view
of their surroundings.

Grizzly relatives

There are seven species of bear alive today, plus the giant panda, which some scientists have classified as a close relative. Apart from the colour of their hair, all bears look very similar, but they occupy different habitats and have very different lifestyles. Grizzly bears usually live in hills and mountains. They prefer mixed habitats that contain woodland, meadow and fresh water. Grizzlies share most of their range with black bears. However the two species rarely meet because black bears are always careful to avoid their larger, more dangerous cousins.

WHAT'S THE DIFFERENCE?

Grizzly bears are much bigger than black bears and are twice as heavy.

●

Grizzlies have an obvious hump on their shoulders, whereas the black bear's back is flat and smooth.

●

A grizzly bear's ears are much shorter and rounder than a black bear's.

◄ Black bears are found over a far greater area of North America than grizzlies. They live in most of Canada and Alaska, northern USA and down the length of the Rocky Mountains almost to Mexico.

The only other bear in North America – the polar bear – lives in the extreme north. Polar bears spend most of their year wandering the sea-ice hunting for seals. In the short Arctic summer, when the sea-ice melts, the bears come on to dry land to eat grass, berries and shellfish. Polar bears never move from the coast.

The grizzly's other relatives live in tropical forests. They include the spectacled bear of South America, the Asian black bear of Central Asia, and the sun bear and sloth bear of Southeast Asia.

▲ The spectacled bear was named after the white marks on its face. Sometimes these marks surround both eyes to look like a pair of spectacles.

A Grizzly is Born

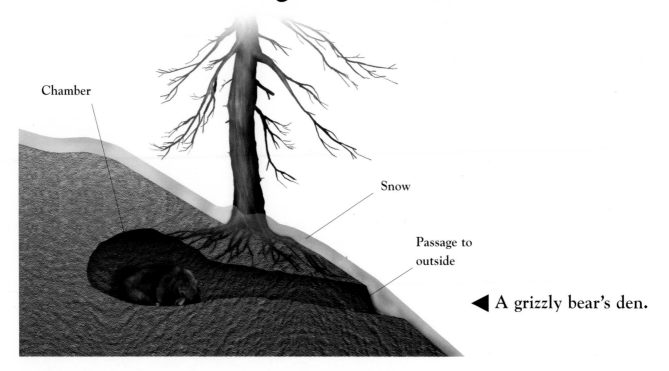

Chamber

Snow

Passage to outside

◀ A grizzly bear's den.

In the depths of a North American winter, a pregnant female grizzly moves uncomfortably inside her den. She is almost eight months' pregnant and about to give birth to cubs.

Grizzly bear cubs are born in a den underground, sometime between January and March. The average litter size is two, but up to four cubs may be born. The female sometimes has difficulty feeding and protecting all the cubs in a large litter. Only the strongest cubs survive longer than the first six months of their lives.

IN THE DEN

It is completely dark inside the den. The young cubs do not see their mother until they are about 15 weeks old, when they leave the den. Instead, they learn to recognize her by smell alone.

At birth the new-born cubs are bald, blind, deaf and completely helpless. When they are hungry, they give out a long, high-pitched squeal until their mother allows them to suckle. The cubs sometimes lie on a soft, warm bed of grass and moss collected by their pregnant mother in the previous autumn.

For the first few months of their lives, the young cubs spend about one hour a day suckling and the other 23 hours sleeping. They grow very quickly, fed constantly by their devoted mother.

▼ At ten days old, grizzly bear cubs still have their eyes tightly closed.

GRIZZLY BEAR CUBS

Grizzly bear cubs weigh less than 450 grams at birth and are about the size of a rat.

●

The cubs open their eyes at about 30 days old and can hear well after 14 days.

Leaving the den

When they are two months old the cubs can shuffle around. As they get bigger, life inside the den becomes more difficult. Soon there is very little room for the mother bear and her cubs.

▼ Male grizzlies are a major predator of bear cubs.

The family must not leave the den too early. They need to wait until the big males have gone to the spring feeding grounds before they emerge. A male grizzly, hungry after five months' sleep without food would probably eat any young cubs he finds. So female bears always stay in their dens for longer than males.

The grizzly cubs first see the outside world at about three months old. By that time they have a thick coat of hair and well-developed hearing and eyesight. They weigh about 9 kilograms when they finally leave the den.

◀ This Alaskan grizzly cub has only recently left the den for the first time.

The outside world

When the cubs first leave the den they are nervous and stay very close to their mother. But as they get older and more confident, they start to leave her side and explore further afield.

▼ Very young cubs grow tired very quickly. This one has scrambled up on its mother's back for a ride.

► Wolves hunt in packs. A grizzly cub away from its mother is an easy target for an animal that can run much faster than an adult bear.

Grizzly bear females are excellent mothers who will defend their cubs against any danger. But the cubs are never completely safe. A young bear that wanders away from its mother's protection might be killed and eaten by a passing wolf or mountain lion.

HUFFS AND GRUNTS

Female grizzly bears and their cubs communicate with calls. Cubs whine and squeal when they are hungry and produce short grunts when they are content. The female gives out a low 'huff' sound to call the cubs back to her.

▲ Female grizzlies spend a lot of time playing with their cubs. This keeps their relationship strong and encourages the young bears to practise their fighting skills.

Mother bears

Mothers with young cubs keep well away from adult male grizzlies, who will eat the cubs given the chance. Even the fresh scent of a male is enough to make a female turn and walk the other way. If they do meet accidentally, a mother grizzly will attack any male that threatens her cubs, even though he may be almost twice her size.

A mother grizzly with young can be one of the most dangerous of all bears. Anyone who accidentally comes between a female and her cubs is in danger of being attacked. This is why it is important to stay well away from bear cubs in the wild. Wherever cubs are found, the mother will always be somewhere nearby.

Female grizzlies are actually frightened of people. They realise that we are the grizzly's greatest enemy so, most of the time, females take great care to keep the cubs away from farms and villages. Even the sound of human voices can make her run.

▼ A young grizzly threatening a larger rival in Katmai National Park, Alaska.

Learning to Survive

One of the first things the young cubs learn once they leave the den is how to avoid enemies. Adult bears can run away quickly, but until they are fully grown, cubs have their own escape technique. When separated from their mother, cubs in danger climb the nearest tree with incredible speed.

Using sharp claws, the cub grasps the tree trunk and pushes itself upwards. In a few seconds it is high up where no large predator can follow. The cub stays in the tree until called down by its mother. Young grizzlies can climb well for the first year of their lives, but they soon become too heavy and clumsy. After the age of 18 months, they will probably never climb another tree again.

▶ Grizzly cubs prefer to climb young trees because they can reach round the thin trunk and hold on tight.

▼ Three cubs wait for their mother at the edge of a lake. Young bears are not always confident in deep water.

16

Fighting and learning

Grizzly cubs spend a lot of time playing and mock-fighting. As they grow older, the fights become very aggressive. The hours spent playing and fighting help build up the cubs' muscles, teach them to defend themselves and sharpen the survival skills they will need later in adult life.

▲ Cubs first start playing while still underground in the winter den where they were born. They continue to play-fight until the family splits up and the cubs become independent.

The cubs also learn by carefully watching and copying their mother. When she stops to sniff a log, so do the cubs. When she stands up on hind legs to look around, the cubs stand up too.

At about four months old the cubs start to eat solid food, including insects and berries, but they still like to suckle milk from their mother as often as she will allow. Throughout the summer they put on up to 15 kilograms of weight every month. The cubs need to build up a thick layer of fat to help them live through the long winter, when they will not have the chance to feed.

▲ This cub is splitting open a rotten log to reach the grubs inside.

GROWTH RATE

A fully grown grizzly bear is 500 times heavier than a new-born cub. Young bears must spend most of their time feeding to achieve this rate of growth.

Independence

Grizzly bear cubs stay with their mother until they are about two or three years old. By this age they have learned how to find a wide range of food and are big enough to defend themselves against most enemies. So their mother decides that her cubs are ready to take care of themselves.

◀ Grizzly cubs rely on their mother for protection and knowledge. They try to stay with her for as long as possible.

▲ Young bears are very vulnerable to predators when they first become independent.

At first the mother bear tries to simply walk away from the cubs. But the young bears have only ever lived with their mother and usually want to stay with her. When she leaves, the cubs trail behind. Eventually the female charges at the cubs to keep them away. If the cubs still follow, the mother will become increasingly aggressive and may even attack them to drive them off. At last, the cubs learn to stay away from their mother. Now they have to survive on their own.

Territory

At first the bear spends its time eating and avoiding larger rivals. It needs to thoroughly explore the landscape, discovering exactly where and when to find food.

▶ Once the grizzly has found a suitable territory, it usually stays there for life.

One of the first challenges for the young bear is to find its own territory. This can be a very dangerous time in the bear's life. As the young animal searches for a suitable area of land, it wanders into the territories of other grizzlies and may be attacked by the adults. The young grizzly is not big enough to fight a fully grown bear. It will be attacked and driven away many times before finding a good area for its own territory.

▲ Newly independent grizzlies must fight off rivals to establish their own territories.

TERRITORY PATROL

A male grizzly patrols a territory of between 500–1,000 square kilometres. The territory of a female ranges between 100–700 square kilometres. Each grizzly covers most of its territory every year.

Finding Food

Grizzly bears are members of the carnivore family. 'Carnivore' means meat-eater, but in practice grizzlies are omnivores, which means they will eat almost anything.

▼ Grizzly bears will investigate anything in search of food. This young cub is learning to use its sensitive nose to find hidden insects.

FAVOURITE FOODS

The young grizzly is an opportunist, who will take food wherever it can be found. A grizzly's favourite meal is sweet food such as honey, or fatty food such as meat. These provide the bear with lots of energy and nutrition. In the spring, the bear will raid birds' nests for chicks or eggs, and it will quickly swallow almost any insect in reach.

GRIZZLY BEAR FOOD CHAIN

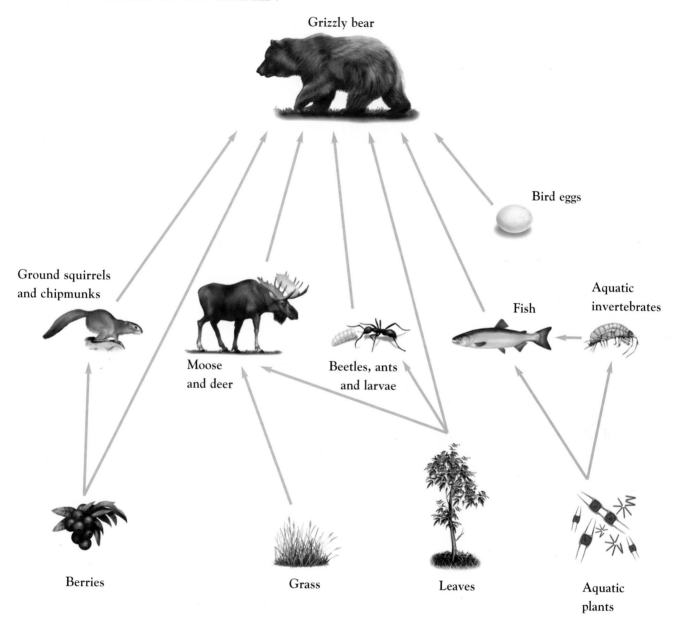

Grizzly bear

Bird eggs

Ground squirrels and chipmunks

Moose and deer

Beetles, ants and larvae

Fish

Aquatic invertebrates

Berries

Grass

Leaves

Aquatic plants

▲ A typical grizzly bear food chain. The bear's exact food depends upon the habitat in which it lives.

A grizzly bear has one of the widest-ranging diets of any living animal. A healthy adult eats up to 16 kilograms of food each day, which can be made up of meat, insects, fish, eggs, roots, berries, leaves and grass.

GRIZZLY TEETH

Bears, just like humans, have a mixture of teeth that are designed for eating meat and chewing plants. Grizzlies have long, sharp canine teeth for killing prey and slicing meat. They also have strong flat molars for grinding leaves and grass.

▲ The grizzly's sharp canine teeth are much longer than the other teeth. These are killing weapons.

Meat

Meat is one of the young grizzly's favourite types of food. It is rich in fat and protein, which are essential for growth and health. The bear will find meat in many different ways. Grizzlies are carrion eaters, which means they will feed from the carcasses of dead animals they happen to find. Some bears have learned to search roads looking for the bodies of animals killed by traffic.

The adult bear will even steal food from smaller carnivores such as coyotes. Its finely tuned sense of smell can pick up the scent of fresh meat up to a mile away. If a group of coyotes kill a deer or other large prey, a grizzly can appear in minutes, moving in to take the meal by force. The bear is so powerful and dangerous that the coyotes simply abandon the food to avoid being hurt.

▼ This single grizzly bear is strong enough to chase away four wolves from the body of a deer they have recently killed.

Hunting

If there is no meat to steal from other carnivores, the grizzly bear has to hunt for itself. First, the bear uses its excellent sense of smell to find animals hiding underground. Then it will use its long, powerful claws to dig deep holes in the earth, hoping to reach the hidden dens of ground squirrels and chipmunks.

▼ Golden-mantled ground squirrels are known as copperheads. They are just one of the many small mammals hunted by grizzly bears.

▲ New-born deer spend their first hours hiding in long grass. Their camouflage is very good, but it is no protection against the sensitive nose of a hungry grizzly.

Sometimes the young bear will turn over rocks in search of worms and beetles hiding underneath. It breaks open rotting logs to eat wood-boring insects and their larvae inside. Ants are a particular favourite. The grizzly will spend a long time carefully scraping open nests to lick up the countless adults and grubs inside.

As it gets bigger, the bear will hunt for larger prey. A single blow from one of its massive front feet can break the neck or back of most animals. When a bear kills large prey, it will eat as much as it needs and then leave the remains covered with branches and leaves. After a sleep somewhere nearby, the grizzly will return for another feast the following day.

◄ A grizzly cub investigates every plant to check if it can be eaten.

Plant food

Meat only provides 5–10 per cent of a bear's diet. The rest is made up of grass, leaves and other plants, and sometimes fish. A grizzly cannot digest thick stems and tough leaves, so it eats only soft, fresh growth. The bear plucks off leaves with surprisingly delicate and sensitive lips. It also digs up roots and wades in water to eat aquatic plants such as horsetails.

As summer slowly turns into autumn, the grizzly abandons grasses and turns to different food. For a short time it feeds from the huge harvest of nuts and berries, which appear throughout most of its territory. Grizzly bears particularly like blueberries and mountain ash berries.

▼ A grizzly bear fills up with crowberries in the last few weeks before winter arrives.

Fishing

Grizzlies who live near rivers where salmon migrate take full advantage of this rich food supply. In spring each year, adult salmon leave the sea and swim upstream, returning to the rivers where they were hatched in order to breed. Positioning themselves beside waterfalls or narrow stretches of river, grizzlies wait patiently until a salmon swims within reach, or leaps up out of the waterfall in order to swim upstream.

Most fish are caught with a quick snap of the jaws. But sometimes the grizzly just stands on a fish and then picks it out of the water with its teeth. In a good year, the bear will catch a fish every few minutes.

▲ Good salmon rivers attract large numbers of grizzlies. This is one of the few times when bears come together in groups.

▶ Sometimes there are so many salmon the bears just have to wait until the fish come to them.

33

Adult Life

In late September and early October, the adult grizzly must build its own winter den for the first time. Some grizzlies use the same den for several years, while others build a new one every winter.

The bear will try to find a remote slope for its den, high up in the hills. Most dens are dug under big trees, where the thick tangle of roots holds the soil together and stops the roof collapsing. There is a diagram of a grizzly den on page 8.

◀ Grizzlies try to move into their dens before the worst winter weather arrives, but when snow falls early the bears may not be ready.

◀ Food is difficult to find in winter. Grass stops growing, insects disappear and many small mammals are in hibernation.

The grizzly scrapes out the earth with its claws and chews through any thick roots in the way. By digging upwards, the bear makes sure the sleeping area is higher than the entrance hole. This traps heat inside the den and stops water trickling in.

When snow starts falling, the bear moves into its den. Once inside, the den entrance is soon covered by a thick layer of snow so a grizzly's winter den is very difficult to find. Soon the grizzly will be asleep.

DEEP SLEEP

The grizzly will sleep underground for about six months, but since their body temperature only drops a few degrees, the grizzlies do not enter deep hibernation. Instead they enter a form of light hibernation called 'dormancy', which is really just a deep sleep.

An animal in true hibernation is almost impossible to wake up, but a grizzly can be woken by a loud noise outside. However, the layer of snow hiding the den helps keep out the noise and insulates the bear from the worst of the winter cold.

Waking up

As winter finally turns to spring, the bear is woken by the rising temperature. Male grizzlies leave their dens in March or April and the females are about one month later. They are all very hungry and immediately start searching for food. The bear's first meal is often the remains of smaller animals that did not survive the winter. Each bear spends the next few weeks eating to build up its strength.

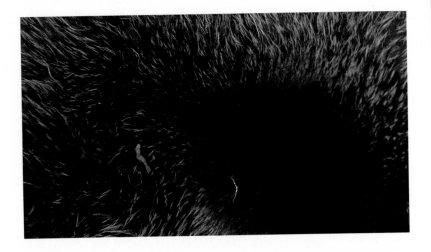

A grizzly bear's thick fur is perfect for keeping out the cold in early spring, but it is far too warm for the sunny days of late spring and summer. A grizzly quickly overheats if it stays out in hot weather, so it spends the summer days sheltering under thick undergrowth and becomes completely nocturnal.

DAYBEDS

On hot summer days, grizzlies make a daybed by digging out a hollow in the soil, or they just doze on a platform of leaves and twigs. Most daybeds are close to good feeding areas and at sunset the bears get up and eat.

◀ This close-up photograph shows the thick fur on the back of a male grizzly.

▶ When the bears wake up in the spring, their food supply has returned.

Finding a mate

At some time over the age of four years old, the grizzly may start looking for a mate. Dominant males in search of females will drive off or even kill any other male they meet. Big males mark their territories by rubbing against trees and rocks, which leaves a strong scent and warns off rivals.

At first a female is very wary of a male, since he is much larger than her and can sometimes be aggressive. The female usually walks away when a male first approaches. But eventually she allows him to come closer and finally they mate.

◄ This bear is scratching its itchy skin against a tree trunk. Bear fur is home to fleas that bite and irritate the skin.

▲ The male bear on the right is much larger than the female.

A male grizzly will stay with a female for up to two weeks and they will mate many times before separating. During the rest of the breeding season, the male may mate with several females.

Although the female will now be pregnant, the cubs inside her do not develop yet. The unborn cubs will not start to grow until the female enters her winter den in November.

BREEDING

Grizzlies mate in June and July. They can start to breed at the age of four years.

●

A female grizzly bear gives birth just once every three years. In her entire life she may only produce eight cubs that reach adulthood.

Threats

Once the grizzly bear is fully grown it has no natural enemies. Humans are its biggest threat. In the past, bears were hunted for meat and for their warm skins. Farmers shot and trapped them to protect livestock and thousands were killed on sight simply because people were frightened.

Today it is illegal to kill grizzly bears. However, licensed hunters are allowed to shoot black bears, and in the gloom of a thick forest, they sometimes kill grizzlies by mistake. Other bears are knocked over by traffic as they cross roads at night.

▲ When facing a dangerous enemy, grizzlies stand on their hind legs to make themselves look bigger. This is no help against a vehicle and every year many bears die in traffic accidents.

ZOOS

Since the population of grizzly bears is so low, most people only ever get to see them in zoos. Bears often breed successfully in zoos and may also live much longer than they do in the wild because they are well-fed and receive medical attention. But some people believe that bears should never be kept in cages. In their native wilderness, bears are free to wander across a huge territory. In a zoo they are confined to just one spot.

Like so many other animals, bears are threatened by the destruction of their habitat. The sheltered valleys where grizzlies spend the early summer feeding are also areas that are ideal for farmers looking for new grazing land. When agriculture invades a traditional feeding ground there is often conflict between bears and humans. The bears are usually driven away and sometimes even killed.

▶ Bears have been kept in zoos for centuries, not always for educational reasons. Two thousand years ago Romans staged brutal competitions where captive bears were forced to fight gladiators and prisoners of war.

41

Grizzlies and humans

Bear attacks are very rare, since grizzlies try to avoid humans wherever possible. Most travellers in bear country never see a grizzly even when they are looking for one. But bears who come into close contact with humans can completely lose their natural fear.

In the past, people were allowed to feed bears in US national parks, and grizzlies learned to expect people to give them scraps. The bears waited to be fed on roadsides and car parks. If food was not offered, the grizzlies would look for it.

◀ Most bears avoid humans. This display of aggression shows that the bear was taken by surprise and is probably very frightened.

HOW TO AVOID A GRIZZLY ATTACK

When walking in bear country, always carry food in sealed containers to reduce the amount of scent.

•

If there are bear tracks, make lots of noise to let the bear know you are there. Then the bear will move away.

•

Never keep food in a tent. It should be stored high up in a tree, well away from the campsite.

▼ Warning signs remind visitors to keep an eye open for bears.

Grizzlies broke into cars and tents to reach picnic baskets, and people in the way were sometimes badly hurt or even killed. Some bears had to be shot for the safety of visitors.

National parks now ban feeding and the grizzlies have lost interest in humans. The number of attacks has dropped and bears no longer need to be killed. Throughout the USA there are many conservation projects designed to help save the grizzly and at last their population is starting to grow again.

WARNING

BEAR

FREQUENTING AREA

Removal of this sign may result in INJURY to others and is punishable by law

THERE IS NO GUARANTEE OF YOUR SAFETY WHILE HIKING OR CAMPING IN BEAR COUNTRY

Grizzly Bear Life Cycle

 **1** A grizzly bear cub is born inside its mother's winter den in January or February. There may be one or two other cubs.

 **2** The bear cub first comes into the outside world at about three months old. The young cub is now covered in thick brown hair, its senses are well developed and it can run and climb.

 **3** At about eight months old the grizzly cub enters its first winter den with its mother. It is still suckling her milk.

 When it reaches the age of three years old, the cub is abandoned by its mother and must look after itself. The first job is to find a suitable territory that the bear will probably keep for the rest of its life.

 Between the ages of four and eight years, the grizzly bear mates for the first time. Male bears mate every year but females breed just once every three years.

 By the age of fifteen years the bear has reached full size and has a well-established territory. The only threats to survival are humans, road traffic and disease. A grizzly bear can live up to 35 years old.

GEOGRAPHY
- Mapwork: where grizzlies live
- Environmental change: destruction of woodland habitat for farming
- Tourism: national parks
- Food journeys

ART
- Shape and movement
- Camouflage

SCIENCE
- Woodland habitat
- Classification: mammals
- Adaptation to habitat: grizzly's body features
- Dormancy and hibernation
- Grizzly's life cycle
- Food chain and pollution

Grizzly Bear Topic Web

HISTORY
- Grizzlies in Ancient Rome

ENGLISH & LITERACY
- Meanings of names: scientific and common
- Write a story about a day in the life of a grizzly cub
- Conservation debates

ICT
- Look at conservation groups' websites
- Send an email to the government expressing a point of view

MATHS
- Grizzly numbers
- Height and weight comparisons

Extension Activities

English
- Debate whether grizzlies should be kept in zoos.
- Find and list collective names for groups of animals, or terms for their young eg cub, calf, chick.

Geography
- Trace a world map from an atlas. Label the continents where the different types of bear live.
- Draw a bear distribution map, showing where each species of bear lives in a different colour.

Art
- Make a food-chain frieze of the grizzly's diet.
- Draw a grizzly warning poster, with tips for survival.

Science
- Make a chart showing how parts of the grizzly's body are specially adapted for certain functions.
- Compare the dormancy of the grizzly with the hibernation of a hedgehog.

Dance and Drama
- Make up a dance that shows a grizzly walking and standing on its back legs.

Glossary

Altitude The height of something, usually above sea-level.

Breed To produce young.

Canine teeth Long, sharp pointed teeth at the front of the mouth used for killing and tearing meat.

Carnivore An animal that eats meat.

Carrion The remains of a dead animal that is eaten by other animals.

Dominant The leading animal in a group, usually the most powerful and aggressive.

Endangered A species whose numbers are low and is in danger of extinction.

Extinction The total disappearance of an entire species.

Habitat The area where an animal lives.

Hibernation Deep winter sleep, when the body temperature drops, and breathing and heart rate slow down.

Litter A group of young animals born at the same time from a single mother.

Molars Large flat teeth at the side of the mouth, used for chewing and grinding food.

Nocturnal To be active at night and sleep during the day.

Omnivore An animal that eats both meat and vegetation.

Prey An animal that is killed and eaten by another animal.

Suckle To drink milk from the teats of an adult.

Territory The area that is controlled and defended by an animal.

Further Information

Organizations to Contact

WWF-UK
Panda House, Weyside Park,
Godalming, Surrey
Tel: 01483 426444
www.wwf-uk.org

Care for the Wild International
1, Ashfolds, Horsham Road
Rusper, West Sussex, RH12 4QX
www.careforthewild.org.uk

Websites

The Bear Den
www.nature-net.com/bears
A site with information about bears and links to other sites.

PBS Nature: Grizzlies of Siberia
www.pbs.org/wnet/nature
The story of raising a pair of grizzly cubs rescued from a Russian zoo.

WWF
www.panda.org/kids/wildlife/mnbrbear.htm
Facts and pictures about bears.

Books to Read

Atlas of Endangered Animals (Belitha Press, 1994)

Country Fact Files: Canada and USA (Hodder Wayland, 1997)

Nature Encyclopedia (Dorling Kindersley, 1998)

Really Wild: Bears (Heinemann, 1996)

What is a Mammal by Robert Snedden (Belitha Press, 1997)

Index

All the numbers in **bold** refer to photographs or illustrations.